The Kingfisher

A Comedy in Two Acts

by William Douglas Home

A Samuel French Acting Edition

New York Hollywood London Toronto
SAMUELFRENCH.COM

Copyright © 1981 by William Douglas Home

ALL RIGHTS RESERVED

CAUTION: Professionals and amateurs are hereby warned that *THE KINGFISHER* is subject to a Licensing Fee. It is fully protected under the copyright laws of the United States of America, the British Commonwealth, including Canada, and all other countries of the Copyright Union. All rights, including professional, amateur, motion picture, recitation, lecturing, public reading, radio broadcasting, television and the rights of translation into foreign languages are strictly reserved. In its present form the play is dedicated to the reading public only.

The amateur live stage performance rights to *THE KINGFISHER* are controlled exclusively by Samuel French, Inc., and licensing arrangements and performance licenses must be secured well in advance of presentation. PLEASE NOTE that amateur Licensing Fees are set upon application in accordance with your producing circumstances. When applying for a licensing quotation and a performance license please give us the number of performances intended, dates of production, your seating capacity and admission fee. Licensing Fees are payable one week before the opening performance of the play to Samuel French, Inc., at 45 W. 25th Street, New York, NY 10010.

Licensing Fee of the required amount must be paid whether the play is presented for charity or gain and whether or not admission is charged.

Stock licensing fees quoted upon application to Samuel French, Inc.

For all other rights than those stipulated above, apply to: International Creative Management, 825 Eighth Avenue, New York, NY 10019.

Particular emphasis is laid on the question of amateur or professional readings, permission and terms for which must be secured in writing from Samuel French, Inc.

Copying from this book in whole or in part is strictly forbidden by law, and the right of performance is not transferable.

Whenever the play is produced the following notice must appear on all programs, printing and advertising for the play: "Produced by special arrangement with Samuel French, Inc."

Due authorship credit must be given on all programs, printing and advertising for the play.

No one shall commit or authorize any act or omission by which the copyright of, or the right to copyright, this play may be impaired.
No one shall make any changes in this play for the purpose of production.
Publication of this play does not imply availability for performance. Both amateurs and professionals considering a production are strongly advised in their own interests to apply to Samuel French, Inc., for written permission before starting rehearsals, advertising, or booking a theatre.
No part of this book may be reproduced, stored in a retrieval system, or transmitted in any form, by any means, now known or yet to be invented, including mechanical, electronic, photocopying, recording, videotaping, or otherwise, without the prior written permission of the publisher.

ISBN 978-0-573-61130-8   Printed in U.S.A.   #627

OPENING NIGHT, DECEMBER 6, 1978

BILTMORE THEATRE

Elliot Martin
with
Hinks Shimberg
in association with John Gale
presents

Rex Harrison Claudette Colbert
George Rose

in

The Kingfisher

a new comedy by
William Douglas Home

Setting Designed by Costumes Designed by Lighting Designed by
Alan Tagg **Jane Greenwood** **Thomas Skelton**

Directed by
Lindsay Anderson

The Producers and Theatre Management are members of
The League of New York Theatres and Producers, Inc.

CAST

(*in order of appearance*)

HAWKINS .... *George Rose*

CECIL .... *Rex Harrison*

EVELYN .... *Claudette Colbert*

The scene is set throughout in Cecil's garden.

The Kingfisher

ACT ONE

SCENE 1

A garden, with a stream tinkling just beyond it, Off Stage. A great beech tree. On the opposite side is a little garden house or shed, in which SIR CECIL WARBURTON *is typing as the Curtain rises.*

All that we see is the open window. HAWKINS, *his butler-valet is arranging tea on a garden table. As he goes into the house to get his last load of equipment, with an empty tray, he knocks on the garden house door.*

HAWKINS. Tea time, Sir Cecil.

CECIL. (*Off.*) Shut up. (HAWKINS *goes on in. A cuckoo calls. The typing goes on.* HAWKINS *comes back. The typing stops.* CECIL *comes out.*)

HAWKINS. How did you get on this afternoon?

CECIL. Not too well. (*He moves to his seat at the tree near the tea table.*) In fact, I'd only just got going when you interrupted.

HAWKINS. My apologies, Sir Cecil.

CECIL. Coleridge had a maid—you know, the poet, Samuel Taylor. And she barged in and said 'Lunch is served', and scuppered Kubla Khan. That's why it's so short.

HAWKINS. Mercifully so, in my view.

CECIL. You're a Philistine.

(HAWKINS *begins to arrange the rug for* CECIL's *legs.*)

CECIL. That's all right, Hawkins, don't fuss.

HAWKINS. Are you sure you'll be warm enough, Sir Cecil?

CECIL. Yes, man, warm as toast.

HAWKINS. You should have settled for tea in the house, Sir Cecil, at this time of year. The summer's not established yet.

CECIL. Rot. It's as warm as toast. There's going to be a heat wave. Said so on the radio at lunchtime. And they look like being right, for once. Remember to put out my summer vest and pants tomorrow.

HAWKINS. Cast no clout, Sir Cecil, till May—

CECIL. Don't be so damned cissy.

(*During all this,* HAWKINS *has been preparing the tea table, and at this point he heads back into the house to get some equipment.* CECIL *fills his pipe, suddenly looks up, drops his pipe, and fixes his gaze on the Off-Stage river, gets up, scattering his rug and taking his field glasses off the back of his chair, and goes over to the river bank and looks upstream.* HAWKINS *enters.*)

HAWKINS. Oh, Sir Cecil, really! I'd just got you settled in your rug.

CECIL. Don't shout, man. It's the kingfisher. He's settled on that post up at the corner. Lovely little creature! Want to have a look?

HAWKINS. (*Taking the glasses, and looking upstream.*) It's gone, Sir Cecil.

CECIL. I expect you frightened it away. Which way did it go?

HAWKINS. Further downstream.

CECIL. Ah, yes. Oh, well, p'raps it'll come back up if we don't chivvy it. (*He returns to his chair, hanging up the glasses again on the chair back.* HAWKINS *picks up the rug and re-arranges it.*) Hawkins.

HAWKINS. Sir Cecil?

CECIL. Have you ever felt the urge for company in your declining years?

HAWKINS. I have the pleasure of your company.

CECIL. No. Female company, you damned fool.

HAWKINS. What's the difference, at our age, Sir Cecil?

CECIL. Speak for yourself!

HAWKINS. Very good, Sir Cecil—

CECIL. Anyway, you never liked them, did you?

HAWKINS. I was fond of dalliance as a young man, Sir Cecil.

CECIL. You're romancing, Hawkins, you're believing things that never happened. (HAWKINS' *brow furrows uncertainly.*)

HAWKINS. It's not easy to distinguish between fact and fiction any more.

CECIL. Why try?

HAWKINS. Yes, why indeed, Sir Cecil.

CECIL. So you think I'm in my dotage, do you?

HAWKINS. Not at all, Sir Cecil. All I'm saying is that to a non-medical eye like my own, it would appear that the first flush of youth has passed you by.

CECIL. But not the second. (HAWKINS *goes on laying the table.*) Did you hear that, Hawkins? Not the second.

HAWKINS. Yes, Sir Cecil.

CECIL. And I'm not referring to my second childhood. I'm referring to my second spring—or is it summer?

HAWKINS. Indian, it could be—

CECIL. Well, it isn't. Just imagine what a summer's like in India. Flies everywhere, and steaming sacred cows with flapping ears, and tigers licking cart tracks of caked mud until their tongues bleed. No, it's spring.

HAWKINS. And when did this condition evidence itself, Sir Cecil, if I might ask?

CECIL. Breakfast time on Monday morning. When I read The Times obituary and saw Townsend, Reginald. If I'd been a bird, I would have started singing. As it was, I whistled in my bath.

HAWKINS. I heard you. But I put it down to general well-being.

CECIL. Well, it wasn't. It was Reggie Townsend popping off. He married Evelyn.

HAWKINS. Evelyn.

CECIL. Evelyn Rivers. Just before your time. The loveliest girl that you ever saw. I kissed her underneath this very beech tree once. Well, more than once. (HAWKINS *goes on arranging the crockery*.) She loved me, Hawkins.

HAWKINS. Naturally, Sir Cecil.

CECIL. But I didn't love her. Can you beat it? Everything the doctor ordered in one lovely girl, with blue eyes and corn-coloured hair under a beech tree. And I put her back.

HAWKINS. A not unknown experience, Sir Cecil.

CECIL. Evelyn sparkled, Hawkins, that's the word I'm looking for. She sparkled like those things that children hold at Christmas. And she made me laugh. I don't remember laughing since.

HAWKINS. Come, come, Sir Cecil.

CECIL. And I put her back! And Reggie hooked her the next day, and landed her. That's when I grew up, Hawkins. Fifty years ago, the morning that I read the paper and saw Reggie Townsend was engaged to Evelyn Rivers. That's what changed my life. Or rather, brought it to a close.

HAWKINS. You've lived life to the full.

CECIL. I haven't, Hawkins. All I've done is stick it between covers. I've not lived, not in the fullest sense. Not yet. Not in the way I should have. But I've got the opportunity at last. That's why I've fixed tea out here, underneath this beech tree.

HAWKINS. So it's Mrs. Townsend coming?

CECIL. No, it isn't, Hawkins. Lady Townsend's coming, on her way back from the funeral. They knighted him for some damned crookery or other in between the wars. As luck would have it, he conked out in Polzeath. He was playing golf. It damn well serves him right, if you ask me, at his age. Showing off, I call it. Anyway, when I wired my condolences, she wired back saying she'd be passing on her way home, and could she stop in for tea. So, now, you're in the picture and you're evidently not mad on it?

HAWKINS. Well, Sir Cecil, with Sir Reginald so recently interred.

CECIL. What's his interment got to do with me?

HAWKINS. It seems a trifle premature, Sir Cecil.

CECIL. Premature? It's fifty years too late!

HAWKINS. Nonetheless, to come straight from the graveyard to tea with an old admirer seems a shade too like Renaissance Italy for my taste.

CECIL. Nonsense, Hawkins. It's the perfect timing. I believe in striking when the iron's hot. And I can't think of any time when it'll be hotter than this afternoon. And she's bound to be emotional—well, isn't she?

HAWKINS. The odds are certainly in favour of it, yes.

CECIL. Well, what could be a better moment? Catch her on the jump and hook her while a man's voice still means something to her.

HAWKINS. Marry her, you mean, Sir Cecil?

CECIL. Why not—if she'll have me? You don't like the idea, do you?

HAWKINS. I'm concerned about your happiness, Sir Cecil.

CECIL. Good—hang onto that. (*A bell rings in the hall.*) Wish me luck, Hawkins.

HAWKINS. Good luck, sir.

CECIL. Thanks. Now then, run along and show her

where I am. Then bring the tea and make yourself scarce.

HAWKINS. Yes, Sir Cecil. (HAWKINS *starts to go.*)

CECIL. Oh, and Hawkins—if she's got a chauffeur with her, fill him up with scones, then cut him through the pack until she wants to push off.

HAWKINS. Very good, Sir Cecil.

CECIL. (*Calling after him.*) And don't come and clear away the tea until I ring. (HAWKINS *goes. We hear the cuckoo again.*) Shut up. (EVELYN *comes through from the house.*)

EVELYN. Cecil.

CECIL. Evelyn. Everything go off alright?

EVELYN. Yes, thank you. What do you mean, Cecil? Wouldn't it have been surprising if it hadn't! Actually, someone did tell me once that they'd been to a country funeral where the bell ringers got tight and thought it was the harvest festival and the bells kept peeling all through the service.

CECIL. You needn't make jokes like that, Evelyn. Let yourself go. Have a good cry. (*He moves away—tactfully—then starts eyeing her.*)

EVELYN. I'm alright, Cecil.

CECIL. You've still got your figure.

EVELYN. Thank you, Cecil.

CECIL. Evelyn, look at me. (*She does.*) You've changed.

EVELYN. So have you.

CECIL. You've lost something.

EVELYN. That's right. I've lost Reggie, Cecil.

CECIL. No, I don't mean that. You're not the girl I held in my arms here in 1927.

EVELYN. Here?

CECIL. Yes. Underneath this beech tree. It's the same one, Evelyn.

EVELYN. So it is, and there's the stream.

CECIL. As you say, there's the stream.
EVELYN. How too extraordinary.
CECIL. It isn't really. I bought up the land when my first book was a success, and built the house.
EVELYN. Why did you choose here?
CECIL. Why not? It's a very nice place.
EVELYN. True enough. And so, I'm not the girl that I was fifty years ago. Is that surprising?
CECIL. I suppose not. No.
EVELYN. And you're not the man who held me, if it comes to that.
CECIL. It always does, they say.
EVELYN. In what way do you find me different?
CECIL. You're tougher.
EVELYN. So's the beech tree, I imagine. So are you, I shouldn't wonder.
CECIL. On the contrary. (HAWKINS *comes in with the tea pot and the hot water.*) Ah, Hawkins. This is Lady Townsend.
HAWKINS. We've already met, Sir Cecil.
CECIL. I know. But this is the formal introduction.
EVELYN. I'm so glad to meet you, Hawkins.
HAWKINS. (*Bows only.*) How d'ye do, my lady.
CECIL. Lady Townsend says that everything went off well, Hawkins.
HAWKINS. So the chauffeur's just been telling me.
CECIL. You've got a chauffeur with you, Evelyn?
EVELYN. Yes. I hope it isn't inconvenient.
CECIL. Not at all, we planned it that way. Hawkins has tea ready for him.
EVELYN. Oh, how very thoughtful of you, Hawkins.
HAWKINS. Not at all, my lady. It's a pleasure.
CECIL. Well, nip off and give it to him, and stop chattering. (HAWKINS *goes.*)
EVELYN. Shall I pour?
CECIL. Why not?

EVELYN. Milk?
CECIL. Yes, please.
EVELYN. Sugar?
CECIL. No, thanks.
EVELYN. Don't tell me you're slimming, Cecil.
CECIL. I'm not slimming. I just don't like sugar.
EVELYN. Reggie loved it.
CECIL. So I should imagine.
EVELYN. What does that mean?
CECIL. Well, he liked the good things of life, obviously. What hole did it happen on?
EVELYN. The seventeenth.
CECIL. Oh, nearly made it. Was he doing a good round?
EVELYN. Twelve over. Not bad, for him. And his tee shot was pin high. It's quite a short hole.
CECIL. Were you playing with him?
EVELYN. No, no. I was playing bridge back in the Clubhouse with the other wives. I'd just gone six No Trumps when the Pro rushed in.
CECIL. Did you make it?
EVELYN. Cecil, you've not changed at all. I'm glad it happened at St. Enedoc because he used to play there as a boy.
CECIL. Did you love Reggie?
EVELYN. What a question!
CECIL. Never mind the question. What's the answer?
EVELYN. Have a scone. You know the answer quite well. Butter?
CECIL. Thank you.
EVELYN. Jam?
CECIL. No, thank you. Don't keep asking silly questions.
EVELYN. You began it.
CECIL. Fifty years with someone that you didn't love. You've weathered it well, Evelyn.

EVELYN. Thank you.
CECIL. Better than the same without someone that you did.
EVELYN. Sorry, I don't follow.
CECIL. Fifty years with someone that one didn't love, like you with Reggie, judging from your general appearance, may be less wearing than fifty years without someone one does love—like me without you.
EVELYN. You're telling me you loved me, Cecil?
CECIL. Yes.
EVELYN. You had a funny way of showing it.
CECIL. Not funny—natural.
EVELYN. For animals, I daresay, but not human beings.
CECIL. Both.
EVELYN. Not if you wanted marriage. You lacked all restraint. You frightened me.
CECIL. I see that, now.
EVELYN. That's why I ran back to the Suttons.
CECIL. I know, and I'm sorry. Jim's still living there, you know—at Sutton Place.
EVELYN. I know—he wired when Reggie died.
CECIL. Oh, did he? Good for Jim.
EVELYN. When did you realise you loved me, Cecil?
CECIL. Following you back to the Suttons.
EVELYN. But you never said so.
CECIL. No, I never got the chance. We played that awful game all evening. Then you went to bed. Then, the next morning—
EVELYN. I'd gone to London.
CECIL. You'd gone to Reggie.
EVELYN. Yes. We got engaged that evening.
CECIL. ..On the rebound?
EVELYN. Cake?
CECIL. Please. Answer, Evelyn.
EVELYN. I have answered.

CECIL. In a thoroughly facetious manner. Was it on the rebound?

EVELYN. Does it matter—now?

CECIL. To me, yes—very much.

EVELYN. Why?

CECIL. Because all my life's been spent on the assumption that it was. That's why I never married. That's why I played fast and loose with women—why I'm where I am now.

EVELYN. Sitting pretty.

CECIL. Sitting lonely—standing by for death, without the least experience of life.

EVELYN. You, Cecil—don't be silly! You—without experience of life! You're the best selling, the most famous author in the British Isles—and you say, without experience of life—

CECIL. Of living, then.

EVELYN. Ah, that's a different thing.

CECIL. Wouldn't Reggie let you see me?

EVELYN. No, I promised.

CECIL. Or write to me?

EVELYN. No, I promised that, too.

CECIL. That explains it. I wrote every day for three years.

EVELYN. Don't I know it.

CECIL. And did Reggie?

EVELYN. Yes. He used to burn them. Wait until he had enough to make a good-sized bonfire in the garden—and then burn them.

CECIL. All unopened?

EVELYN. All except one.

CECIL. And who opened that one?

EVELYN. I did.

CECIL. What did it say?

EVELYN. That you wanted me to run away with you.

CECIL. They all said that.

EVELYN. I think this must have been the first one.
CECIL. Why?
EVELYN. Because it gave the time and place and date.
CECIL. Victoria—the boat train platform—9:15 a.m. on May 10th.
EVELYN. That's right.
CECIL. It was the first one.
EVELYN. Were you there?
CECIL. Yes. I was. Where were you?
EVELYN. In Ullapool.
CECIL. Where's that?
EVELYN. In Scotland. We were fishing. At least Reggie was. And I was walking through the heather, thinking.
CECIL. Of what?
EVELYN. You. How long did you wait?
CECIL. Till the train went.
EVELYN. Then what did you do?
CECIL. I got a refund on the tickets.
EVELYN. More tea?
CECIL. No, thanks. Then you started breeding.
EVELYN. Yes.
CECIL. How many did you notch up?
EVELYN. Two. To make sure of security of tenure. And to stop you tempting me away from Reggie.
CECIL. Did he ever talk about me?
EVELYN. Not if he could help it. Only when your first book came out.
CECIL. What did he say then?
EVELYN. He said that it confirmed his worst opinions of you.
CECIL. Literally speaking?
EVELYN. No, no. He conceded that the style was quite good. But he didn't like the content.
CECIL. I don't blame him.

EVELYN. He assumed the bore that she rebounded onto in the second chapter was himself.

CECIL. He was quite right.

EVELYN. And that the girl was me.

CECIL. Right, too.

EVELYN. And that the young man who seduced her was yourself.

CECIL. With licence.

EVELYN. I should hope so. Underneath a beech tree, near a stream, of all the cheek. Just think of the discomfort! Beech mast, sticks and baby thistles.

CECIL. Don't forget they had a rug.

EVELYN. We didn't.

CECIL. What a lot we missed!

EVELYN. You're just a dirty old man! I've heard the expression often, but I've never seen it in the flesh before.

CECIL. I'm just a dreamer, Evelyn.

EVELYN. Nonsense.

CECIL. Dreaming of what might have been, if I'd played my cards right.

EVELYN. If you'd played them right, you would have married me.

CECIL. That's what I wanted.

EVELYN. Nonsense. What you wanted was a good affair. The only thing I'd guess that ever meant a thing to you as far as women are concerned. And you didn't want marriage, so please don't pretend you did.

CECIL. I did. And I'll prove it to you.

EVELYN. How?

CECIL. By asking you to marry me now.

EVELYN. That proves nothing.

CECIL. It proves everything.

EVELYN. It doesn't. It's the only thing you can ask now.

CECIL. Don't you believe it.

EVELYN. Don't be silly, Cecil. Be your age. It's out of reach, that aspect of the matter. Gone beyond recall. So we're down to second best. And I'm not playing.

CECIL. Second best?

EVELYN. Yes. What's the use of asking me to marry you now? It's like giving somebody an empty boiled-egg shell for breakfast, it's a favorite joke with children— But not very popular with grown-ups.

CECIL. I thought that you loved me.

EVELYN. So I did. But not enough to put your slippers out, and knit your pullovers. That isn't what I dreamed about for fifty years.

CECIL. You can't have really loved me, then.

EVELYN. I did. I loved you day in, day out, till it nearly drove me mad.

CECIL. I loved you in the same way.

EVELYN. Well, you should have shown more self-control.

CECIL. Please don't rebuke me, Evelyn. I can't bear it.

EVELYN. I think I'd better go.

CECIL. No, don't go, Evelyn. Please don't go. Stay here the night—a few days. Stay and see if you could bear to stay here always. You could have a free hand in the garden—and the house. You could refurnish it, according to your taste—re-do it altogether. I'm well off. Extremely well off. I'd give you a free hand.

EVELYN. No, thank you, Cecil. It's too late. I'm sorry but it's fifty years too late. The young man who was lying underneath this beech tree fifty years ago, was quite a marriageable proposition. Well, comparatively speaking. You were arrogant, of course, and cynical and irresponsible. But you were honest, at least. Flora was the trouble, wasn't she?

CECIL. That was before I met you.

EVELYN. She was most attractive wasn't she? I'm

surprised she didn't come and see you when her husband died.

CECIL. She did.

EVELYN. Did you ask her to marry you?

CECIL. Yes.

EVELYN. And you say you've always loved me!

CECIL. I thought Reggie was immortal.

EVELYN. What was her excuse?

CECIL. The same as yours. That it was fifty years too late.

EVELYN. And what about the Paris woman?

CECIL. So you know about her?

EVELYN. It was in the papers.

CECIL. So it was.

EVELYN. She shot herself.

CECIL. She missed.

EVELYN. What was her name?

CECIL. You tell me.

EVELYN. Yvette—Yvette something.

CECIL. That's right.

EVELYN. A bit of luck for you, that—wasn't it?

CECIL. You mean that she missed me as well?

EVELYN. No. That she didn't kill herself. You would have been in trouble.

CECIL. Not at all. I thought so at the time, I must admit. I panicked for a moment, but if women go round shooting themselves just because they fall in love, it's really up to them—one can't be held responsible.

EVELYN. Have you seen Yvette since then?

CECIL. Yes. She came here seven years ago. Her husband had just died.

EVELYN. You seem to do a thriving line in widows. Did she turn you down, too?

CECIL. Yes, indeed she did.

EVELYN. The same excuse?

CECIL. Precisely.

EVELYN. I'm not sorry. Yvette rather shocked me, if you must know. Not herself, I mean, the melodrama.

CECIL. And the bullet only missed me by a bee's wing. Hawkins told me—he worked out the angles. You're not armed, are you? Except with integrity!

EVELYN. You're still as irresponsible as ever, Cecil. You're still prepared to pay a compliment, and carry on outrageously at the same time.

CECIL. I haven't been outrageous.

EVELYN. No! You sit there asking me to marry you, and then, without a blush, you tell me that you've done the same thing to two other women when their husbands died.

CECIL. What's that but honesty?

EVELYN. For one thing, it's bad manners.

CECIL. Not at all. You must remember that I'm getting on. I have to take my chances when they come. For all I know, old Reggie might have gone on playing golf till Kingdom come. Well, he did, didn't he? So, you can't blame me, can you?

EVELYN. I'm not blaming you. I'm merely telling you it isn't any use.

CECIL. Because it's fifty years too late?

EVELYN. Yes.

CECIL. Not because you don't still love me.

EVELYN. I must go.

CECIL. Go? Why the devil did you come here then?

EVELYN. (*Gets up.*) To have a cup of tea. How do we get hold of the chauffeur?

CECIL. I'll ring for Hawkins. (*He rings a hut bell.*) It was sex in fact, on your side. And once that was over, well, it wouldn't have worked anyway.

EVELYN. What makes you think so?

CECIL. Well, your present attitude. If you'd really loved me, then you would have married me.

EVELYN. You never asked me.

CECIL. Yes, I did. Just now.

EVELYN. Oh, Cecil—can't you understand—don't go on so. (HAWKINS *enters.*)

HAWKINS. You rang, Sir Cecil?

CECIL. Yes. Has Lady Townsend's chauffeur had his tea?

HAWKINS. He's waiting by the car, my lady.

EVELYN. Thanks, Hawkins. Well, goodbye, Cecil.

CECIL. Goodbye, Evelyn.

EVELYN. Don't get up. And, thank you for the tea.

CECIL. Thank Hawkins, not me. He prepared it.

EVELYN. Thank you, Hawkins.

HAWKINS. Not at all, my lady. It's been a great pleasure.

CECIL. Show her to the car, now, Hawkins.

HAWKINS. Yes, Sir Cecil. Follow me, my lady, please. (*He goes.*)

CECIL. Perhaps we'll meet at Wimbledon, or somewhere, Evelyn.

EVELYN. Perhaps.

CECIL. Anyway, I'll write to you. The chances are they might get read, now.

EVELYN. They might, Cecil.

(*She goes, and* CECIL *sits listening to the sounds of departure.* HAWKINS *returns.*)

HAWKINS. Time you went in now, Sir Cecil. Nearly News time.

CECIL. I'm alright, don't fuss. She turned me down, flat.

HAWKINS. So I should imagine, sir.

CECIL. I'm not much of a proposition these days, am I, Hawkins?

HAWKINS. Neither of us are at our age.

CECIL. We are not discussing you that I'm aware of.

HAWKINS. Naturally not, Sir Cecil. (*He moves to-*

wards the house again, puts down his load and returns to collect more.)

CECIL. No need to get huffy.

HAWKINS. I'm not in a huff, Sir Cecil.

CECIL. Fifty years ago, I could have asked a question, Hawkins, underneath this tree, and changed the course of my life.

HAWKINS. So I understand, Sir Cecil.

CECIL. Why didn't I, Hawkins?

HAWKINS. No doubt, Providence stepped in and saved you!

CECIL. Providence!

HAWKINS. That's what I said, Sir Cecil.

CECIL. Saved me! You said that as well.

HAWKINS. I did.

CECIL. From what?

HAWKINS. May I speak openly?

CECIL. Why not?

HAWKINS. Saved you from the most formidable lady that I've met since I entered your service. I'll put your slippers by the television set, Sir Cecil.

(*He goes.* CECIL *looking straight ahead, then stoops to undo his rug with a view to going in.* EVELYN *appears.*)

EVELYN. Cecil, I've come back.

CECIL. Why?

EVELYN. I can't bear the thought of going back and facing Reggie's golf clubs in the hall. Anyway, it's a woman's privilege to change her mind.

CECIL. I don't advise it. You were right to turn me down. I'm an immoral, dirty, old man.

EVELYN. I'm not arguing.

CECIL. And you're a prim old widow, with a sentimental streak that's temporarily overcome your natural frigidity.

EVELYN. I daresay.

CECIL. And the two don't go together. Not for long, at any rate.

EVELYN. Well, it won't be for very long.

CECIL. Could I have that in writing!

EVELYN. On the wall, yes, Cecil—it's already there.

CECIL. It's coming back, old girl.

EVELYN. What's coming back?

CECIL. The sparkle, I was telling Hawkins just before you turned up, about how you used to sparkle.

EVELYN. What a tiresome girl I must have been.

CECIL. You were enchanting. (HAWKINS *returns*.)

HAWKINS. Pardon me, Sir Cecil, but the chauffeur wants to know if Lady Townsend's staying.

CECIL. For a short time, Hawkins, yes, she is. She'd better have the Blue Room.

HAWKINS. Very good.

CECIL. You'll like that, Evelyn. It looks up the river.

EVELYN. That sounds charming, Cecil.

CECIL. Take her up and show it to her, Hawkins.

HAWKINS. Very good. But what about the chauffeur?

CECIL. Shove him in the pub for tonight, Hawkins. Alright by you?

EVELYN. Perfect, Cecil.

HAWKINS. Follow me, my lady. (*They go. We hear the cuckoo go "Cuckoo, Cuckoo."*)

CECIL. Shut up, Reggie!

THE CURTAIN FALLS

ACT ONE

SCENE 2

HAWKINS *is arranging a tray with bottles on it.* EVELYN *comes out of the house, at her convenience.*

EVELYN. Good evening Hawkins.
HAWKINS. Good evening my lady. What would you like?
EVELYN. What's the most convenient, Hawkins?
HAWKINS. Well, Sir Cecil likes to have a sidecar.
EVELYN. Bless my soul, are they still going? I've forgotten what they taste like.
HAWKINS. Very satisfactory, my lady.
EVELYN. Alright, Hawkins. I'm in your hands. (*He starts to mix her one. She looks round the area, and her eye lights on the garden house.*)
EVELYN. Is Sir Cecil still writing?
HAWKINS. Yes, indeed, my lady, since he only writes about the past. And that's as clear as crystal to him still. To both of us, I'm glad to say. It's just the present that he finds a problem.
EVELYN. What's he working on now?
HAWKINS. A new novel. It's called *"Underneath the Beech Tree."* It's a sequel to an earlier work.
EVELYN. Have you read it?
HAWKINS. I've glanced at it, yes, my lady.
EVELYN. Tell me what it's about, Hawkins.
HAWKINS. I'd rather leave that to Sir Cecil, if you don't mind.
EVELYN. Then I'll tell you. It's about me.
HAWKINS. Your guess is as good as mine, my lady.
EVELYN. What a diplomat you are. How long have you been with Sir Cecil, Hawkins?
HAWKINS. It'll be fifty years next year.
EVELYN. Good Heavens. That's a long time. Where did you meet?
HAWKINS. In the south of France, my lady. I was valet to Sir Christopher Lloyd Hastings, and Sir Cecil —well, of course, he wasn't sir in those days, just plain Mr. Cecil—came to stay. Sir Christopher was interested in young literary talent, and Sir Cecil's first book "Rosemary" had just been published.

EVELYN. I remember.

HAWKINS. Naturally you would.

EVELYN. Why do you say that?

HAWKINS. Well, assuming that you were the prototype of Rosemary, my lady, and Sir Cecil, Jasper.

EVELYN. He's told you that, has he?

HAWKINS. No, my lady. I put two and two together, that's all. After what he said this afternoon.

EVELYN. What did he say this afternoon?

HAWKINS. He told me that you would be here for tea, and he remarked that he had kissed you underneath this beech tree fifty years ago.

EVELYN. What else did he say?

HAWKINS. That he'd put you back.

EVELYN. Put me back?

HAWKINS. It's a term employed by anglers, my lady.

EVELYN. That implies that he'd caught me, Hawkins?

HAWKINS. That's what I assumed, my lady.

EVELYN. Well, he hadn't.

HAWKINS. No, my lady?

EVELYN. No. He hooked me, yes, but when he tried to strike, I wriggled off before the barb went in.

HAWKINS. I see.

EVELYN. Well, don't forget it!

HAWKINS. He went on to say that he regretted losing you acutely.

EVELYN. Did he really say that?

HAWKINS. Yes, my lady.

EVELYN. But he didn't tell you that things didn't happen like they did in the book?

HAWKINS. No, my lady.

EVELYN. Well, they didn't, Hawkins. You can take my word for that.

HAWKINS. Things very seldom do.

EVELYN. Forty nine years. So you must have met

him the next summer. Who was he with in the south of France?

HAWKINS. Sir Christopher Lloyd Hastings, as I said. He was invited for Sir Christopher's stepdaughter, Sheila.

EVELYN. What was she like?

HAWKINS. Blonde, petite, and pretty as a picture.

EVELYK. How old?

HAWKINS. Eighteen—nineteen.

EVELYN. Poor child! Did she manage to get off, like I did?

HAWKINS. No, my lady. In her case, the barb went right in.

EVELYN. And Sir Cecil landed her?

HAWKINS. He did, my lady.

EVELYN. And then put her back?

HAWKINS. Alas, no, she expired, my lady—on the bank.

EVELYN. You mean she died?

HAWKINS. Yes. That same summer.

EVELYN. How dreadful! What from?

HAWKINS. She was "used," my lady—

EVELYN. In what way, Hawkins?

HAWKINS. Sir Cecil was in and out of poor Miss Sheila's bedroom window every night, m'lady, like a cuckoo in a clock, but not so noisy.

EVELYN. How do you know?

HAWKINS. I observed the damage to the bougainvillea each morning, when I laid the breakfast on the terrace.

EVELYN. How long did this go on?

HAWKINS. Until Sir Cecil met another lady—once again, at dinner with Sir Christopher. In fact, Sir Christopher had asked her quite deliberately. She was a well-known courtesan, my lady, Austrian, Countess von Hornstein.

EVELYN. Married?

HAWKINS. Nominally. The Count, I understand, preferred his town house in Vienna and the Spanish Riding School instructors. She was in her early forties, I would think, my lady.

EVELYN. Pretty?

HAWKINS. Beautiful, my lady. Quite outstandingly so. With a most imposing list of lovers. Kings and ex-kings, cinema stars, Russian emigres, French politicians, even Sheiks, I understand. I saw the start of it at dinner —I was serving— And Miss Sheila saw it, too—and left the table in tears.

EVELYN. I don't blame her.

HAWKINS. Then Sir Cecil raised his glass, my lady, to the Countess with a wink, then drank her health. Then he invited her to drive to the Casino in his open touring Bentley.

EVELYN. I see it all! It's like a Philip Oppenheimer. Go on, Hawkins.

HAWKINS. Well, Miss Sheila saw them going from the window of her bedroom, on the second floor. And as the motor car turned right onto the Middle Corniche, she jumped. I can see it now. She landed on the terrace at her Mother's feet, as she was pouring out the coffee. Death was instantaneous, I'm glad to say.

EVELYN. Poor child, how dreadful!

HAWKINS. It was very disconcerting. Then Sir Cecil turned up at the funeral, my lady, bold as brass.

EVELYN. He had the nerve to come!

HAWKINS. Oh, yes, indeed, with a big wreath of bougainvillea, and bearing the inscription "To my darling Sheila, with undying love from Cecil." It caused quite a rumpus, as a consequence of which I came into Sir Cecil's service when Sir Christopher passsed on. That very same day.

EVELYN. The same day! What do you mean?

HAWKINS. Sir Christopher slipped up and struck his

head against a tombstone, during a brawl with Sir Cecil in the graveyard.

EVELYN. What about?

HAWKINS. Miss Sheila's demise.

EVELYN. Rather late then wasn't it?

HAWKINS. Indeed, my lady. But there was a mistrial blowing. They went at it hammer and tongs. Sir Christopher ran at Sir Cecil with a raised umbrella, shouting "I'll get you for this, you young bounder," and then started beating him about the head. Sir Cecil raised his knee and struck Sir Christopher in the crotch, and then when Sir Christopher lurched forward with a strangled cry Sir Cecil hooked him in the hock and down he went! It was the neatest thing I ever saw. He asked me if I'd like to be his valet when he came out.

EVELYN. Out of what?

HAWKINS. Out of prison, M'lady?

EVELYN. How long did he get?

HAWKINS. He didn't go in.

EVELYN. He didn't?

HAWKINS. The French Maitre defending him said that Sir Christopher would have deserved the sentence, had the Almighty not seen fit to impose his own eternal punishment. It sounded better, of course, in the French.

EVELYN. And you went to him at once?

HAWKINS. That very same day, yes, my lady.

EVELYN. Where?

HAWKINS. Countess von Hornstein's villa.

EVELYN. How long did you stay there?

HAWKINS. Till we left for Cairo. And Sir Cecil met the belly dancer.

EVELYN. Belly dancer!

HAWKINS. La Belle Fatima—she was a household name in Cairo in those days. (CECIL *comes in, in a velvet dinner jacket.*)

CECIL. I'm sorry I'm late. Couldn't find my slippers.

HAWKINS. They were in your dressing room, Sir Cecil.

CECIL. No, they weren't. They were on my feet. (*As* HAWKINS *starts mixing his sidecar.*) Do you get like that, Evelyn?

EVELYN. No.

CECIL. You will. You've got it coming to you. Everybody does, when they start going back.

EVELYN. What an expression.

CECIL. I find it descriptive.

EVELYN. I find it depressing.

CECIL. Why? It's natural. They issued us with return tickets when we came into this world, remember? Now we're on the way back. And, soon, we'll hit the buffers, crash-bang—

EVELYN. Don't!

CECIL. Why not? One may as well face facts. The only truth in life is death.

EVELYN. You might as well say that the only truth in death is life.

HAWKINS. You'll pardon me for saying so, it could be wiser to avoid the subject altogether.

CECIL. You keep out of it.

HAWKINS. Apologies, Sir Cecil.

EVELYN. I think you're quite right Hawkins. (HAWKINS *hands* SIR CECIL *his sidecar.*)

CECIL. What are you on, Evelyn?

EVELYN. Same as you.

CECIL. You didn't have to.

EVELYN. I quite like it.

CECIL. Have another one, then. Get her ladyship another sidecar, Hawkins.

HAWKINS. Very good, Sir Cecil.

CECIL. What have you been gossiping about, you two? I heard it from my dressing room.

HAWKINS. Her ladyship was asking how I came to you, Sir Cecil.

CECIL. Was she? And he told you, did he?

EVELYN. He did, Cecil, yes.

CECIL. Trust him—the damned old windbag! Fill me up, too, Hawkins. (*While he is pouring.*) When're you going to learn to keep your mouth shut, Hawkins, eh?

HAWKINS. When the Almighty stops it with the good red earth, Sir Cecil, I imagine.

CECIL. Roll on that day! Go and get the dinner dished up.

HAWKINS. Very good, Sir Cecil. (*He goes.*)

CECIL. (*After a pause.*) To your blue eyes, Evelyn.

EVELYN. (*Raising her glass.*) "To my darling Sheila with undying love from Cecil."

CECIL. So he told you about that, too?

EVELYN. He did.

CECIL. Poor girl. You could say she was my Reggie.

EVELYN. Not as Hawkins just described her.

CECIL. On the rebound, I mean. Sheila was my attempt to scotch the disappointment and frustration of your not being at Victoria Station.

EVELYN. And Countess von Hornstein!

CECIL. Who told you about her?

EVELYN. Hawkins.

CECIL. I don't know why I keep that fellow.

EVELYN. I do. No-one else would stand your bestial behaviour!

CECIL. Bestial!

EVELYN. Yes, there's no other word for it. Just like a badger killing for the fun of it. Hen feathers flying everywhere—then silence in the morning, and no eggs.

CECIL. I didn't kill the countess—we just fell apart. I wish there had been silence in the morning, Evelyn, and at night. I never knew a woman talk so much, that's why I left her.

EVELYN. Then you went to Cairo.
CECIL. Did I?
EVELYN. Hawkins said you did.
CECIL. That's right. We both did.
EVELYN. You and Hawkins?
CECIL. That's right. We went up the Nile. Another sidecar?
EVELYN. Thank you, Cecil. Where you met the belly dancer?
CECIL. (*Stopping.*) Belly dancer! Fatima, you mean.
EVELYN. I wouldn't know. And how long did you stay with her?
CECIL. Till custom staled her infinite variety. And so it went on. But I didn't love them—any of them.
EVELYN. But you loved me.
CECIL. Passionately.
EVELYN. Then why didn't you propose?
CECIL. I did.
EVELYN. Not marriage, Cecil. Why not marriage?
CECIL. I was young, and not quite certain of myself.
EVELYN. You didn't seem that way to me.
CECIL. Evelyn, you know that weekend we first met at Sutton Place. (*He changes the subject, and gets away with it.*)
EVELYN. Yes.
CECIL. Do you know I didn't want to go.
EVELYN. You were asked for Prudence, I suppose.
CECIL. Quite right. A sweet girl but she never would've launched a 1,000 ships. She'd've sunk the lot.
EVELYN. I didn't want to go because I wanted to play golf with Reggie.
CECIL. Well, why didn't you?
EVELYN. Because my Mother didn't want me staying the weekend with him because his parents were away.
CECIL. And Mother didn't trust you?
EVELYN. Evidently not.

CECIL. You mean to say you found Reggie attractive?
EVELYN. He was kind.
CECIL. That's not an answer.
EVELYN. It's the only one you're going to get.
CECIL. (*After a pause.*) I didn't want to come because I wanted to go sailing.
EVELYN. Who with?
CECIL. Flora.
EVELYN. What did she know about sailing?
CECIL. Nothing.
EVELYN. Still she cooked the dinner, I suppose, and made the bed?
CECIL. Precisely.
EVELYN. So you came down to the tennis court at Sutton Place and saw me being beaten six love by Jim.
CECIL. And I fell in love with you on the spot. Then I asked you to walk up the river, after tea. We found a moorhen's nest, remember?
EVELYN. That's right. It was floating. And you told me that they almost always made them like that in case of a flood. It had five eggs.
CECIL. That's right. And then we saw a kingfisher.
EVELYN. Yes, I remember. It flew out from under the bank.
CECIL. Then we both climbed down to see if we could find its nest.
EVELYN. You did. I jumped and landed in your arms, and nearly knocked you over backwards.
CECIL. That was when I kissed you for the first time.
EVELYN. And we didn't find the nest.
CECIL. The bank was too hard. They like sand. They can't dig in it, otherwise. They bore a hole with their beaks, you know.
EVELYN. So you told me.
CECIL. I've heard people say they kick off from the other bank, and hit the sand head first.

EVELYN. You told me that, as well.

CECIL. That's why they need it soft.

EVELYN. Yes, I can understand that.

CECIL. Otherwise, if it was hard mud, or stones, they'd break their necks.

EVELYN. Yes, Cecil.

CECIL. A damned risky business. Thank God I'm not a kingfisher! I saw it just before you came this afternoon.

EVELYN. I know, you told me.

CECIL. Lovely little creature! Say they breed their first year—barring accidents, of course—it ought to be the fortyninth descendant of the one that we saw. That's a thought, eh?

EVELYN. Isn't it, indeed!

CECIL. Another sidecar?

EVELYN. Well, a very little one.

CECIL. (*Over by the tray.*) And then we took our shoes and stockings off, and paddled upstream.

EVELYN. And I hit my toe against a pebble.

CECIL. Yes.

EVELYN. And you took out your handkerchief and dried it. And then kissed it better. Then we paddled on again. Until we got here. Then you said, "Let's climb out and sit underneath that tree." And we did. Then you dried my feet again.

CECIL. They were the smallest feet I ever saw.

EVELYN. They're bigger now.

CECIL. Not much.

EVELYN. Of course they are. Colossal—**Reggie** always used to say how big they were.

CECIL. Oh, good for Reggie! (*Pouring.*) Say when.

EVELYN. When.

CECIL. And you had a mole behind your left knee.

EVELYN. That's right.

CECIL. Is it still there?

EVELYN. I believe so. I've not looked for thirty years.
CECIL. May I look, Evelyn?
EVELYN. No.
CECIL. How long did we stay under that tree?
EVELYN. Nearly three hours. We were late for dinner. Then we played a dreadful word game, after dinner—
CECIL. Then you went to bed and all we dared to do was shake hands.
EVELYN. Prudence came up with me.
CECIL. Don't I know it. I could hear you talking through the wall for hours. What did you tell her?
EVELYN. Everything. Girls do, you know. They like second opinions.
CECIL. And what was your joint conclusion?
EVELYN. That you didn't love me. Prudence said you wouldn't have done what you did, if you had.
CECIL. She was dead wrong, Evelyn.
EVELYN. So you say.
CECIL. How could you listen to her?
EVELYN. Easily. Because she'd had experience.
CECIL. I don't believe it. Who was the shortsighted fellow?
EVELYN. Reggie.
CECIL. Reggie!!
EVELYN. Yes. He'd done the same to her.
CECIL. Good heavens—when?
EVELYN. The week before, at Swinley Forest—in the heather. At the 12th hole. They were looking for his ball.
CECIL. And did they find it?
EVELYN. Don't be flippant, Cecil. That's what made me marry Reggie.
CECIL. I don't get you.
EVELYN. Well, he hadn't done it to me.
CECIL. What chance had he had, good heavens!
EVELYN. Quite a lot, at dances, and at weekends and in people's gardens.

CECIL. Gardens don't have heather. If you'd gone to Swinley Forest with him, he'd have had a go all right.

EVELYN. I lay awake all night.

CECIL. Why?

EVELYN. Thinking about you, and hoping you'd come in. Then I got up early the next morning, and went up to London. And went straight to Reggie's house. His parents were away and he was still in bed. Like you were, I imagine.

CECIL. No, I wasn't. I came down to breakfast early, specially to see you, but you'd gone.

EVELYN. You could have followed me.

CECIL. I didn't know you'd gone, then, I thought you were breakfasting in bed.

EVELYN. No, not me. Reggie was though. So I went up to his bedroom and I said 'Now, look here, Reggie. What's all this that Prudence Sutton told me last night?'. 'What did Prudence tell you?' he asked, blushing like a beetroot. 'About Swinley Forest' I said. 'Oh, that,' he said, getting even redder. 'Listen, Reggie,' I said, 'If I'd come to Swinley Forest with you this weekend would you have done the same to me?' 'Of course not, Evelyn,' he said.

CECIL. Bloody liar.

EVELYN. 'Why not?' I said. 'Because I respect you,' he said.

CECIL. Sanctimonious prig!

EVELYN. Cecil, be quiet. Now I've forgotten where I'd got to.

CECIL. Reggie was respecting you.

EVELYN. Yes, that's right. Then I said 'Prove it,' 'How the devil can I?' he said. 'Easily,' I said, 'I'm getting into bed with you right now.' 'Good God!' he said, 'I haven't had my egg yet.' 'Never mind that,' I said, 'Give me that tray.' Then I put it on the bedside table.

CECIL. Wait a minute, Evelyn. How the devil did you manage that?

EVELYN. Manage what, Cecil?

CECIL. Putting the tray on the bedside table. When I try that lark, it's always cluttered up with telephones and books and lamps and ashtrays and alarm-clocks. Not the tray, old girl, the bedside table—don't misunderstand me.

EVELYN. Do you want to hear the story of my life or don't you, Cecil?

CECIL. Yes, please.

EVELYN. Well, shut up about the tray then. Take it from me—it was on the bedside table.

CECIL. Right.

EVELYN. And then I started to undress.

CECIL. Good heavens!

EVELYN. That's what Reggie said. Then I went on undressing.

CECIL. Bless my soul!

EVELYN. Then Reggie said, 'I'd rather marry you, old girl, to tell the truth.' 'I don't believe you,' I said. 'It's the truth,' he said. And so we got engaged. And then I ate his egg.

HAWKINS. (*Comes in.*) Dinner is served, Sir Cecil.

CECIL. Thank you, Hawkins. (HAWKINS *retires.*)

EVELYN. What are you thinking, Cecil?

CECIL. Nothing.

EVELYN. Come along. I'm your guest and I want to know.

CECIL. When you ate Reggie's egg—where were you? In bed?

EVELYN. No, of course not.

CECIL. Why not?

EVELYN. Because Reggie was a gentleman.

CECIL. (*Put out by this.*) Straight up the steps and through the hall and just right.

CURTAIN

ACT TWO

SCENE 1

The time is after dinner. Late night. HAWKINS *is taking off the coffee tray, leaving the brandy and the crème-de-menthe.* CECIL, *perhaps in a velvet smoking jacket, is smoking a cigar.*

CECIL. Hold on a minute, Hawkins. Evelyn? Breakfast?
EVELYN. Toast and marmalade, please, Cecil—that's all.
CECIL. Tea, or coffee?
EVELYN. Coffee, please.
CECIL. (*As* HAWKINS *turns away.*) You're sure you wouldn't like it upstairs?
EVELYN. No, no, Cecil. I'm an early riser. Always have been. Reggie found it very irritating.
CECIL. Did he really? Nine o'clock then, Hawkins—downstairs.
HAWKINS. Indoors, or out here?
CECIL. Out Hawkins, if it's fine.
HAWKINS. Very good, Sir Cecil. The barometer seems set fair.
CECIL. Alright, Hawkins, you can fall out now.
HAWKINS. Goodnight, Sir Cecil.
CECIL. 'Night.
HAWKINS. Goodnight, my lady.
EVELYN. Goodnight, Hawkins. Sleep well. (HAWKINS *goes. After a short pause.*) Cecil, what was Hawkins like when he first came to you?
CECIL. Blue eyes—fair hair, and eye-lashes like garden rakes.

EVELYN. Were you in love with him?
CECIL. A little.
EVELYN. Actively?
CECIL. Good heavens, no. We used to swim together in the moonlight now and then, that's all.
EVELYN. How democratic of you.
CECIL. I was young then, Evelyn. Anyway, what's so wrong? Women haven't a monopoly of beauty. Hawkins in those days was an Adonis—like that statue southeast of Hyde Park, whose arse you drive at coming down Park Lane.
EVELYN. Cecil!
CECIL. I'll bet you've looked at Rodin's lovers in your time—and not been too particular about which one you looked at.
EVELYN. I know which you look at, Cecil. Yvette, Fatima and Flora and a regiment of others I dare say.
CECIL. Yes, legions of them. I plead guilty, but I couldn't help it. Once I had become a literary lion, they headed for my bed like wasps towards a jam pot. It was quite amazing, Evelyn, when you come to think of it. Some weeks I'd chalk up five or six—or even seven. Sometimes, double figures. After lunch, and after tea and after dinner, and another one at bedtime. Frequently, I called them by the wrong names. I got so confused.
EVELYN. Did all this overtime improve your work.
CECIL. Of course not. But it dulled my memory of you. More crème-de-menthe?
EVELYN. Why not?
CECIL. Good girl. (*He goes to the tray.*)
EVELYN. Are you still on overtime these days, Cecil?
CECIL. Good God, no. I'm totally quiescent now. Have been for seven years. (*He has handed her her refilled glass, refilled his own, and settled in his chair again.*) At least I think I am after what happened down

in Cornwall, actually. At the St. Mawes Hotel. You know it?

EVELYN. Yes, of course. We often stayed there.

CECIL. You and Reggie?

EVELYN. Yes.

CECIL. Why?

EVELYN. To play golf at St. Austell.

CECIL. That's right. We drove past the course.

EVELYN. Who's we?

CECIL. Louise de Noialles.

EVELYN. French again, I take it.

CECIL. Half Moroccan. Big black eyes and flashing teeth. And patches of scrub everywhere—

EVELYN. How old?

CECIL. Too young for me. And Mother Nature evidently knew it, so she went on strike.

EVELYN. It must have been embarrassing.

CECIL. It was—and damned expensive.

EVELYN. Do you mean she was a courtesan?

CECIL. Good heavens, no, of course not. But I had to see it through. She had been looking forward to it. We played Scrabble instead.

EVELYN. In the bedroom?

CECIL. Anywhere it took our fancy, in the bath, one evening. And I had the faucet end.

EVELYN. You're a fighter, Cecil, I'll give you that.

CECIL. I never felt so silly in my life. Like a nude bank clerk in a hold up.

EVELYN. Which night was that?

CECIL. Saturday.

EVELYN. What did you do on Sunday?

CECIL. Scrabble. Then we went to watch the cormorants coming in to roost across the bay. They dived in like that Batman fellow in the cartoon, down between the cliffs, like darts. Then sat up looking like a row of crazy ink bottles.

EVELYN. And did she like that?

CECIL. No, not much. The wind was in the east. We packed it in at tea time. And she caught the sleeper up to London.

EVELYN. Have you seen her since?

CECIL. No.

EVELYN. Poor old Cecil. Are things still like that, do you suppose?

CECIL. I haven't tried to find out.

EVELYN. Why not?

CECIL. Because the right person hasn't been around.

EVELYN. Still dreaming, Cecil?

CECIL. Old men dream dreams—specially old bachelors, Evelyn.

EVELYN. You can't bring dreams to reality, though, Cecil.

CECIL. Have you ever tried to?

EVELYN. Once, with Reggie's A.D.C. I fell in love with him in Cairo. He looked just like you, and he behaved like you exactly. Terribly attractive. I dreamed of him quite a lot in the hot weather. Then, one day, I told him—or night, rather. At a party, after too much champagne.

CECIL. How long did it last?

EVELYN. Till he came back to England on leave—the same time as I did, when my daughter had mumps at school very badly. But he wouldn't let me near him after I'd been to see her. Then he married a girl in the Wrens when he got back to Cairo. And I had to sit and listen to him saying, "With my body I thee worship."

CECIL. Poor old Evelyn.

EVELYN. I think Reggie understood. He passed me a huge handkerchief in church, and then he stood beside me right through the reception. And I cried myself to sleep for nights and nights.

CECIL. And what did Reggie do about that?

EVELYN. Stroked me on the bottom, and then turned his back and went to sleep.

CECIL. And where's the fellow now?

EVELYN. They live just outside Wolverhampton.

CECIL. Have you seen him since?

EVELYN. No.

CECIL. Poor old Evelyn.

EVELYN. Don't keep saying that.

CECIL. Well, what else can I say?

EVELYN. Say he was just a flash in the pan. Reggie was much kinder and more stable.

CECIL. (*Repeating.*) He was just a flash in the pan. Reggie was much kinder and more stable.

EVELYN. And worth six of him.

CECIL. Of course he was. He kept you happy, Evelyn.

EVELYN. No, he didn't. Never, for one minute. Not in fifty years. Oh, I know he was kind. But I just didn't love him.

CECIL. Yet you had two children.

EVELYN. Yes, I know.

CECIL. How did you manage that?

EVELYN. I shut my eyes and thought of you.

CECIL. Or Reggie's A.D.C.

EVELYN. I hadn't met him then.

CECIL. What are the children like?

EVELYN. Jack's got his father's stammer. Otherwise, he's more like me.

CECIL. Blue eyes—and fair hair?

EVELYN. More or less. What's left of it.

CECIL. Married?

EVELYN. Yes.

CECIL. Who to?

EVELYN. A girl called Barbara. Well, she's not a girl—not anymore.

CECIL. Good looking?

EVELYN. Yes.

CECIL. Make Jack a good wife?
EVELYN. First class.
CECIL. Good. How many children?
EVELYN. Three girls.
CECIL. Blue eyes and fair hair?
EVELYN. No. All dark.
CECIL. Oh, what went wrong?
EVELYN. Nothing. Barbara's Chinese.
CECIL. What about the other one—the daughter.
EVELYN. Harriet. She's married to a bishop in South Africa.
CECIL. How many children?
EVELYN. None. The bishop's impotent.
CECIL. Oh, well, one can't have everything. Did they know you were coming here?
EVELYN. No.
CECIL. Why not?
EVELYN. They don't know I know you, and I thought they might be shocked.
CECIL. What by?
EVELYN. Me coming straight here from the funeral. Let alone stay the night.
CECIL. You'll have to marry me now, Evelyn, you've been compromised.
EVELYN. What nonsense! I'm of age. Besides I'm free. It's only just dawned on me.
CECIL. That's the spirit, Evelyn. Have a mouthful more.
EVELYN. If you will.
CECIL. I will.

(*This makes* EVELYN *think of* REGGIE *again.*)

EVELYN. Do you think Reggie's got to Heaven yet?
CECIL. I haven't thought about it. Even money, I'd say.

EVELYN. Do you believe in God?

CECIL. At times.

EVELYN. What do you mean by that?

CECIL. Clough.

EVELYN. Clough?

CECIL. Arthur Hugh, the poet. (*Quoting.*)
"And almost everyone, when age
  Disease or sorrow strike him,
  Inclines to think there is a God,
  Or something very like him."

EVELYN. So you do believe now age has struck you?

CECIL. Yes.

EVELYN. And what about when sorrow struck you?

CECIL. When you married Reggie, you mean? No. I was too young. I thought *He* was a bastard.

EVELYN. Just supposing Reggie's got there, Cecil, what do you suppose he's doing?

CECIL. Don't ask me.

EVELYN. I like to think he's playing golf with people like Napoleon.

CECIL. Did he play?

EVELYN. I don't know. Cecil, you might not get in because of Sheila.

CECIL. Sheila?

EVELYN. The girl who committed suicide.

CECIL. There's not a word of truth in all that, Evelyn.

EVELYN. But you told me—so did Hawkins.

CECIL. Yes, I know. But we invented it. So long ago that we believe it now. But it's not true.

EVELYN. You mean that you invented Sheila?

CECIL. That's right.

EVELYN. And the Countess?

CECIL. Yes.

EVELYN. And all the others?

CECIL. Yes.

EVELYN. You don't expect me to believe that, do you?

CECIL. Yes! If you try very hard.
EVELYN. Including Fatima?
CECIL. Yes, I invented the lot.
EVELYN. Really?
CECIL. All, except Louise de Noialles.
EVELYN. So she's true?
CECIL. Yes. She's the only one that is.
EVELYN. Oh, Cecil!
CECIL. But it's not her name.
EVELYN. What is it, Cecil?
CECIL. I'm not telling you.
EVELYN. That isn't fair. I told you about Roger.
CECIL. That's a different thing. The point is that we only weakened once, each, during fifty years.
EVELYN. Except for Reggie.
CECIL. I'm not counting him. He was your husband.
EVELYN. That's broadminded of you.
CECIL. We've been faithful, Evelyn, in our different fashions. There's no doubt about it. That could bode well for the future. Don't you think so?
EVELYN. If there is one.
CECIL. What does that mean?
EVELYN. Anno domini.
CECIL. Well, what about it, Evelyn?
EVELYN. What about what?
CECIL. Marriage.
EVELYN. Give me time to think about it, Cecil.
CECIL. How long?
EVELYN. A few minutes. Oh, I don't know, Cecil.
CECIL. Is there anybody else?
EVELYN. Yes.
CECIL. Who?
EVELYN. Jim.
CECIL. Who's Jim?
EVELYN. Jim Sutton. He wired me like you did—after Reggie died. He asked me first, in fact.
CECIL. Asked you what?

EVELYN. If I'd marry him.
CECIL. What? In the telegram?
EVELYN. No, that weekend in Sutton Place.
CECIL. And you said no.
EVELYN. I said I'd think about it.
CECIL. Did you?
EVELYN. Yes I did and I still might.
CECIL. You haven't seen him lately?
EVELYN. No.
CECIL. I saw him last week. At the Parish Council Meeting. Looking dreadful. Walking on two sticks, if you can call it that. Acute arthritis in both hips.
EVELYN. Why don't they operate?
CECIL. They reckon he's too old.
EVELYN. He's younger than you.
CECIL. Not much.
EVELYN. At least a year.
CECIL. He doesn't look it.
EVELYN. I'll have to take your word for that.
CECIL. And, anyway, I haven't got arthritis.
EVELYN. You're jealous, Cecil!
CECIL. Don't be so damned silly. How could anyone be jealous of a human wreck like Jim? He's practically on all fours—one foot in the grave, if he could get it that far!
EVELYN. Yes, I've got the message, Cecil.
CECIL. And he's damn near broke. He never knew the first thing about farming. Even though he was the Minister of Agriculture in the Middle Ages. God Almighty, have you got no judgment, Evelyn, no discernment?
EVELYN. Jim proposed to me, I can't forget that, Cecil. And you didn't.
CECIL. I have now.
EVELYN. That's true.
CECIL. A nightcap?

EVELYN. Are you going to have one?
CECIL. Yes.
EVELYN. What?
CECIL. Whiskey and plain water.
EVELYN. Alright.
CECIL. What about it, Evelyn? Is there still hope for me?
EVELYN. Where would we live?
CECIL. Here.
EVELYN. Why not in my house?
CECIL. I like this one.
EVELYN. There's no room for Jack and Barbara and the children . . .
CECIL. Thank God.
EVELYN. There you are, you see. Just thinking of yourself.
CECIL. I'm not. I write well here. That's why I want to stay here.
EVELYN. So your writing comes before me?
CECIL. Naturally. I've got to keep you, haven't I?
EVELYN. No. Reggie left me quite a lot of money.
CECIL. How much?
EVELYN. Plenty. And a great big house with a delightful study. And a swimming pool. And fallow deer.
CECIL. I don't swim. And I don't shoot.
EVELYN. Don't be silly, Cecil. They're ornamental deer. And as for swimming, you should. I do. Twice a day. Just wait till I tell Hawkins that. We could go in together, while you cooked the breakfast in the morning, and shook up the cocktails in the evening.
CECIL. You're being most amusing, Evelyn.
EVELYN. Thank you. And I've got a sauna.
CECIL. I don't like them.
EVELYN. Nor did Reggie. But I made him have them. I think that's what killed him. He had one the day before we went to Cornwall. And then we played croquet after dinner, and the wind was in the east.

CECIL. I hope you told the Coroner that.

EVELYN. No, I didn't. What's a sauna got to do with playing golf?

CECIL. You heard about the golfer who died on the 14th fairway, miles away from anywhere? The fellow he'd been playing with brought him back to the clubhouse, and the Secretary congratulated him and said that he must have found it very tiring, "I did," said the fellow. "What with putting him down and then picking him up again after every shot."

EVELYN. I don't think that that's very funny, Cecil, in the circumstances.

CECIL. Well, it wouldn't have been funny if it'd been in any other circumstances, would it?

EVELYN. What's the time?

CECIL. Half past eleven.

EVELYN. Is it really? It's miles past my bedtime.

CECIL. Nonsense. The night's still young.

EVELYN. (*Getting up.*) Not for me, it isn't, Cecil. I'm an early bedder, so if you'll excuse me.

CECIL. Have one for the stairs?

EVELYN. No, thank you.

CECIL. Come along, I'm going to.

EVELYN. No, I've had too much already. Goodnight, Cecil. (*She moves towards him, holding out her hand, and then trips slightly.*)

CECIL. (*Leaping up.*) Steady on, old girl. (*He supports her.*)

EVELYN. You see, I'm tipsy.

CECIL. No, you're not. It's just the ground. It's bumpy.

EVELYN. Thank you, Cecil. (*She goes on.*)

CECIL. Evelyn.

EVELYN. (*Stopping.*) Yes?

CECIL. Come over here with me.

EVELYN. Where to?

CECIL. (*He holds out a hand. She comes back. He takes her over, and then stops.*) Now, stand there while I get the rug. (*He goes and gets it.*)

EVELYN. The moon's up.

CECIL. I know. It's brand new, too.

EVELYN. You ought to turn your money, oughtn't you?

CECIL. I've not got any on me. You turn Reggie's! (*He has returned with the rug to the grassy slope by the tree.*)

EVELYN. Please stop talking about Reggie, Cecil.

CECIL. All right, that's a bargain. I'll drop Reggie from my conversation, if you'll drop Jim Sutton—done?

EVELYN. Done.

CECIL. Now then— (*He throws down the rug.*) that's where we were sitting. Sit down, Evelyn, there.

EVELYN. Whatever for?

CECIL. Sit down and you'll find out.

EVELYN. Cecil!

CECIL. Go on. Don't be so damned coy. I'll help you. (*He takes her hand and helps her lower herself onto the rug.*) Well done. (*He starts lowering himself.*)

EVELYN. Careful, Cecil. Don't strain anything. (*With her help, he too, gets down.*)

CECIL. Thanks, Evelyn. (*They sit together.*) Listen to the water.

EVELYN. Peaceful, isn't it?

CECIL. I was on this side, wasn't I?

EVELYN. I think so, yes. So far as I remember. (*Another long pause.*)

CECIL. Evelyn.

EVELYN. Yes, what is it, Cecil?

CECIL. The same proposition that I put to you at tea time. But this time, I want an answer. Not a string of hypothetical excuses. Will you marry me?

EVELYN. Yes, Cecil.

CECIL. Thank you. (*He takes her hand and kisses it.*)

EVELYN. What a sentimentalist you are.
CECIL. It did the trick, though, didn't it?
EVELYN. Yes, I suppose so. Now I'm off to bed. Give me a shove. (*She puts her hands on his shoulders, and tries to raise herself.*)
CECIL. I can't from here.
EVELYN. Well, move round then.
CECIL. I can't.
EVELYN. Yes, of course you can. (*They move back to back.*)
CECIL. Now.
EVELYN. It's no good.
CECIL. Try it this way. (*He gets on hands and knees.*) That's better. Put your hands on my shoulders. (*She does.*) Up she comes!
EVELYN. She doesn't, Cecil—that's the trouble!
CECIL. Let me have a go. (*He starts trying to get up.*) You give me a shove.
EVELYN. You're too heavy, Cecil.
CECIL. O.K. We'll have to call in reinforcements. Hawkins! Hawkins! (*He either crawls over to, or reaches for, the Convent Bell, and rings it.*) He'll be asleep, the old fool!
EVELYN. We'll have to spend the night here. (*He peals it again.*)
CECIL. Suits me. (*He peals again.*)
EVELYN. Hawkins, Hawkins. (HAWKINS *appears in a dressing gown.*)
HAWKINS. Did you call, Sir Cecil?
CECIL. Ah, good man. You heard us, did you, Hawkins?
HAWKINS. Yes, Sir Cecil. I was on my way down to the cellar.
CECIL. What for?
HAWKINS. I've mislaid the key, I thought it might be in the lock.
CECIL. Come over here.

HAWKINS. (*On his dignity.*) What is it you require, Sir Cecil?
CECIL. Help, you bloody old fool. Get hold of my hands and pull me up. Come on. (HAWKINS *takes his hands.*) Don't be a cissy—pull, man, pull.
HAWKINS. (*When he's up.*) You're sure you won't need helping with her ladyship.
CECIL. No, I can manage. Well, you'd better hang around, just in case.
HAWKINS. Very good, Sir Cecil.
CECIL. Come on, old girl. (*He holds her hands.*) Up you come. (*She rises, but not enough.*) Bring up the reserves, Hawkins.
HAWKINS. Yes, Sir Cecil. (HAWKINS *gets behind him, and they both pull. She comes up.*)
CECIL. Thank you, Hawkins. (*After an exchange of looks with* EVELYN.) I imagine you're wondering why we got down there, Hawkins.
HAWKINS. Not at all, Sir Cecil. It's not my place.
CECIL. Don't be so damned pompous.
HAWKINS. I'll say goodnight, my lady.
EVELYN. Goodnight, Hawkins.

(*He starts again for the house, ignoring* CECIL, *but is stopped by the latter's intervention.*)

CECIL. Hold on, Hawkins. I'll tell you. It was my idea, and it worked. We're engaged—I said we're engaged.
HAWKINS. In that case, I must ask you to accept a fortnight's notice.
CECIL. Don't talk rot, man.
HAWKINS. It's not rot, Sir Cecil. It's straight from the heart.
CECIL. Then I suggest you go to bed and sleep it off.

(HAWKINS *goes.*)

EVELYN. He meant it, Cecil. Poor old man!

CECIL. Don't worry about him. He's had too much port! (*She notes his irritation and his worry, just as he has noted hers.*)

EVELYN. Oh dear, it's spoilt everything!

CECIL. Rot. Just forget it. I've forgotten it already.

EVELYN. Have you really, Cecil?

CECIL. Yes, completely.

EVELYN. Goodnight, Cecil.

CECIL. Goodnight, Evelyn. Sleep well. (*This time, he kisses her on the cheek. She goes towards the house, and he stands looking after her. Calling after her.*) Evelyn, if there isn't a hot water bottle in the Blue Room holler down the stairs.

EVELYN. (*Voice off, from the house.*) Don't bother, Cecil.

CECIL. (*Calling.*) It's no bother. And the sheets may be damp. (*He stands there, thinking his own thoughts, then he puts a glass or two on the tray and picks it up to take it in.* HAWKINS *comes out.* HAWKINS *takes the tray without a word and goes.*)

EVELYN. (*Voice calling from the window of the Blue Room.*) Cecil—

CECIL. (*Answering.*) Yes?

EVELYN. (*Voice off.*) There isn't a hot-water bottle.

CECIL. No? I'll bring one up, old girl. (*He goes in.*)

THE CURTAIN FALLS

ACT TWO

SCENE 2

The Curtain rises on HAWKINS *laying the breakfast.* HAWKINS *taps the door.*

HAWKINS. Breakfast time, Sir Cecil. (HAWKINS *goes. A cuckoo calls. Then it stops and* CECIL *enters, pours his coffee, sits down and picks up* The Times *and starts to read it.* EVELYN *comes in.*)

EVELYN. Am I late?

CECIL. (*Rising.*) No, just right.

EVELYN. Don't get up. (*She goes for her coffee.*)

CECIL. Good morning, my dear.

EVELYN. (*Keeping her distance.*) Morning, Cecil.

CECIL. What's the matter?

EVELYN. Nothing. Isn't it a lovely day.

CECIL. Yes. Warm as toast. (CECIL, *a little put out, resumes his seat. She joins him at the table.*)

EVELYN. There any news?

CECIL. Not much. It says you buried Reggie. And there's an obituary.

EVELYN. Who by?

CECIL. Anonymous.

EVELYN. Long or short?

CECIL. Short. You'd better read it. (*He holds out the paper.*)

EVELYN. Read it to me, Cecil.

CECIL. Nothing to it. It just says he conked out playing golf in the West Country. Born in 1900. Knighted in between the Wars. That you've survived him and two children.

EVELYN. Is that all?

CECIL. Yes. What else did you expect?

EVELYN. I don't know. But it's so impersonal.

CECIL. (*His edginess beginning to get the better of him.*) I reckon that he's lucky to get in at all. There's dozens like him pop off every day of the week.

EVELYN. Reggie was my husband, Cecil.

CECIL. Yes, I know. But he meant damn all to the chap who wrote that notice. Churns out hundreds of them every year, I shouldn't wonder. Soul-destroying job.

EVELYN. I think he might have mentioned what he did for Padstow.

CECIL. What did he do for Padstow?

EVELYN. Gave them a sports ground.

CECIL. Did he? Good for Reggie. But you can't expect a thing like that to be of universal interest. Too parochial. Jim Sutton gave a swimming pool to Honiton, but who the hell cares?

EVELYN. Quite a lot of children, I imagine.

CECIL. Yes, but they don't read the *Times*. (*He turns to another part of the paper.*) I think they've done him proud, considering.

EVELYN. Considering what, Cecil?

CECIL. That he was as dim as they come. (*There is a pause, while they continue with their breakfasts.*) Well, I've got my book to finish. That'll take another three weeks at the outside. What about the first of next month?

EVELYN. What for, Cecil?

CECIL. Booking up the vicar.

EVELYN. Cecil I'm not going to marry you.

CECIL. You're not—!

EVELYN. I mean it, Cecil, I'm afraid.

CECIL. But it was all fixed up last night. We got engaged, remember?

EVELYN. Yes, I know we did. But I'd had a lot of crème de menthe. And you'd had a lot of brandy.

CECIL. I was sober as a judge. The crème de menthe's just an excuse. And a damned bad one, too. It's something else. I know, you're annoyed by what I just said about Reggie.

EVELYN. No, it's not that.

CECIL. Well, what is it, then?

EVELYN. Don't keep on asking questions, Cecil.

CECIL. Why? I want to know why, Evelyn. After all we supped the wine of paradise together last night.

EVELYN. Never ask a woman for a reason, Cecil.

CECIL. Got it! Hawkins giving in his notice last night. That's it, isn't it? You think I can't get on without him, don't you?

EVELYN. I'm quite sure you can't.

CECIL. Ah, there you are! I knew it!! That old bugger's wrecked the whole caboodle.

EVELYN. No, he hasn't Cecil.

CECIL. Well, who has?

EVELYN. It's time I went and packed.

CECIL. Packed! You're not going!

EVELYN. Yes, I must.

CECIL. Why?

EVELYN. They expect me home.

CECIL. You're going straight home?

EVELYN. Very likely.

CECIL. To the golf clubs in the hall.

EVELYN. Maybe I'll have to learn to live with them. (HAWKINS *comes in with his tray.*) Good morning, Hawkins.

HAWKINS. Good morning, my lady. (EVELYN *goes.*)

CECIL. Morning, Hawkins.

HAWKINS. Good morning, Sir Cecil.

CECIL. Lovely day. It's all off, Hawkins so you needn't go on sulking.

HAWKINS. Why is that, Sir Cecil?

CECIL. Mind you own damned business!

HAWKINS. (*Still lingering.*) I hope it's not to do with anything I said last night.

CECIL. Good God, so you remember last night, do you?

HAWKINS. Naturally, Sir Cecil.

CECIL. That surprises me. You were as pissed as a newt.

HAWKINS. Nonetheless, I recollect the incident with total clarity.

CECIL. Then you should be ashamed.

HAWKINS. I am, Sir Cecil—deeply.

CECIL. That's a likely story! You're so damned jealous, you're thrilled there's been a bust up. And you know it.

HAWKINS. That assessment of the situation would have been entirely accurate last night, Sir Cecil, as I was drink taken. Not this morning, though, I've sobered up now.

CECIL. Who cares? It's too damned late.

HAWKINS. Surely not, if you allow me to withdraw my ultimatum.

CECIL. You don't think we've broken our engagement just because you handed in your notice, do you?

HAWKINS. It occurred to me.

CECIL. Then you're flattering yourself, old chap.

HAWKINS. I wonder.

CECIL. Well, stop wondering, for God's sake. Who the devil do you think you are?

HAWKINS. The only person in the world that you can't live without, Sir Cecil.

CECIL. Balls to that! and balls again!

HAWKINS. (*Turning away.*) If that's your attitude, there's no more to be said.

CECIL. Yes, there is—a mouthful. (HAWKINS *stops.*) And I'm going to say it now. And you're going to listen. Put the bloody tray down, and stop fiddling about! (HAWKINS *puts the tray down, and turns back to face him.*) Let's get one thing straight, Hawkins, here and now. Because you've been with me for fifty years, it doesn't mean that I can't do without you. In fact, I've a damned good mind to hold you to your word, and be rid of you in a fortnight's time.

HAWKINS. I wouldn't advise that, Sir Cecil.

CECIL. I don't give a damn what you advise. It's what I want that matters. Not what you want. And I'm fed up with you! You're a petulant old bitch, if you want my opinion. When I get engaged to someone who I've been in love with all my life, what do you do? Congratulate me? Not at all. You stick your bloody little oar in, thinking only of yourself, and bugger up the whole works.

HAWKINS. So it was to do with me, Sir Cecil—as I thought. I'm sorry.

CECIL. It was not to do with you. And it's no damned good being sorry. It's done now.

HAWKINS. Not were I to withdraw my notice, surely?

CECIL. Don't keep talking like a bloody parrot. Push off, I can't stand the sight of you.

HAWKINS. That being so, I'll let my notice stand.

CECIL. What makes you think I'd dream of letting you withdraw it? You're not the only pebble on the beach. There's lots more like you. Geriatrics, swilling their employers' port down like a mouthwash. They're all over the country. Thousands of 'em. But, repulsive as they are, I doubt if any of them are as unattractive as you—or as pompous.

HAWKINS. You'll regret those words.

CECIL. I couldn't care less.

HAWKINS. Then I'll be leaving in a fortnight, as I said, Sir Cecil. (*He starts to go.*)

CECIL. (*Shouting after him.*) You can go now, if it suits you better. It suits me fine. (HAWKINS *checks as he receives this body blow and goes without the tray.* EVELYN *comes in.*)

EVELYN. What's wrong with poor Hawkins?

CECIL. I've just given him the sack.

EVELYN. I thought he sacked himself last night.

CECIL. He tried to take it back just now. I wouldn't let him.

EVELYN. Why not? Now I'm going home.

CECIL. Because he's wrecked my life.

EVELYN. He hasn't, Cecil, don't be silly. I'm the one

who might do that, not Hawkins, if I made the wrong decision.

CECIL. If you loved me like I love you, you'd make the right one.

EVELYN. You may love me, Cecil, but do you love marriage? Or are you a loner? With your books, your butler and your selfishness.

CECIL. I've lost my butler, now.

EVELYN. You'll get him back. Don't worry. All you've got to do is ask him.

CECIL. I'll be damned if I'll do that.

EVELYN. Then I'll ask him for you.

CECIL. No, I hate his guts. I'd like to push him in the river.

EVELYN. You'll get over that.

CECIL. If Hawkins stayed on, would you marry me?

EVELYN. Don't go on so, Cecil. You're giving me a headache. (*A pause.*)

CECIL. What will you do in Andover?

EVELYN. Play bridge and weed the garden.

CECIL. And swim.

EVELYN. Yes, and swim.

CECIL. And have your sauna baths.

EVELYN. That's right.

CECIL. Be careful in them. I knew somebody who got stuck in one, once. Old Richardson. He used to be a Colonel in the Blues. The wood swelled on the door when he was inside, and he couldn't open it. His wife came down to feed the ponies, luckily. He's never touched a lobster since, they tell me. (HAWKINS *comes in, dressed for the road in a sports coat over his normal dark trousers.*)

HAWKINS. I'm just off, Sir Cecil.

CECIL. Off—where are you going to?

HAWKINS. Reading, Sir Cecil.

CECIL. What the devil do you want to go to Reading for?

HAWKINS. I have a widowed sister living there.

CECIL. You gave a fortnight's notice. You can't go yet.

HAWKINS. You said it'd suit you fine if I went now, Sir Cecil. (*He turns to* EVELYN.) I was wondering if I could get a lift with you as far as Andover, my lady?

EVELYN. Cecil, go away.

CECIL. Where to?

EVELYN. I want to talk to Hawkins.

CECIL. Do you want the *Times*?

EVELYN. No, not now.

CECIL. May I take it?

EVELYN. Yes, of course.

CECIL. It helps. (*He goes off with the* Times.)

EVELYN. I'm sorry that you've quarreled with Sir Cecil, Hawkins.

HAWKINS. So am I, my lady. But I can't stay with him. He said dreadful things. I can't forget them.

EVELYN. Nonsense.

HAWKINS. No, my lady. My mind's made up. I can't stay with him another day. He said such terrible things.

EVELYN. He was angry, Hawkins. So he didn't really mean them.

HAWKINS. I'm afraid he did, my lady. And he's never said them before—not in fifty years.

EVELYN. Said what, for heaven's sake?

HAWKINS. He called me an old bitch, my lady. (EVELYN *fights against a smile.*)

EVELYN. That was unkind.

HAWKINS. But that's not the worst of it. He said that I was unattractive. There—I've told you now.

EVELYN. And you feel better, don't you?

HAWKINS. No, my lady.

EVELYN. You will, when I tell you something, Hawkins. We discussed you quite a bit last night.

HAWKINS. You did.

EVELYN. Yes, and Sir Cecil told me that you used to swim together in the moonlight.

HAWKINS. Yes, that's right.

EVELYN. And he said that you were an Adonis—like that statue south-east of Hyde Park whose ar— (*She checks and rephrases just in time.*) who's got his back towards Park Lane.

HAWKINS. I know the one, you mean my lady.

EVELYN. Well, he likened you to that, so it's not really likely that he thinks you're unattractive, is it? Well then, pull yourself together. Don't be such a silly-billy.

HAWKINS. But I still don't understand, why he became so rough with me all of a sudden.

EVELYN. Well, you gave your notice in.

HAWKINS. I know, that, but I tried to take it back this morning. But he wouldn't listen. All he said was, "It's done now. It's over." Might I ask if that would be correct, my lady.

EVELYN. I don't know.

HAWKINS. Although you've loved him all your life.

EVELYN. Yes, Hawkins. Just as you have. I don't think I've had one waking moment when I haven't thought of him in the last fifty years. But love's one thing. And marriage is another. Or a different kind of love, at any rate.

HAWKINS. How true.

EVELYN. You've learn't that, Hawkins, haven't you?

HAWKINS. At long last, yes, my lady. (*She allows her mind to dwell on* REGGIE *for a moment, and then she looks up.*) Please stay, Hawkins.

HAWKINS. Very good, my lady.

EVELYN. Thank you.

HAWKINS. Thank you, my lady.

EVELYN. Hawkins.

HAWKINS. Yes, my lady?

EVELYN. Do you think that Captain Sutton is at home?

HAWKINS. He is, my lady, yes.
EVELYN. Will he be there now?
HAWKINS. Yes, my lady. He'll be schooling horses.
EVELYN. Schooling horses—is that wise?
HAWKINS. My lady?
EVELYN. It's not too much for him?
HAWKINS. No, my lady. He's extremely fit for his age.
EVELYN. Oh! When the car comes, will you give the chauffeur my bags. And tell him to come and pick me up at Sutton Place. (*Gives pound note.*)
HAWKINS. Thank you, my lady.
EVELYN. Can I get to Sutton Place along the river path still?
HAWKINS. Yes, my lady.
CECIL. (*Coming on.*) The all-clear gone yet, Evelyn?
EVELYN. Yes—we've finished talking, Cecil.
CECIL. Good—Damned difficult today, this bloody puzzle.
HAWKINS. Would you like your rug, Sir Cecil?
CECIL. No, thanks. It's much warmer out here than it is inside. (EVELYN *nods dismissal, and* HAWKINS *goes.*)
EVELYN. Hawkins'll stay with you, Cecil.
CECIL. Has he said so?
EVELYN. Yes.
CECIL. How did you bring him round?
EVELYN. By kindness.
CECIL. I'm not sure I want him.
EVELYN. Don't be horrid, Cecil. Hawkins loves you.
CECIL. Good God!
EVELYN. And he's always loved you. Ever since you took him swimming in the moonlight.
CECIL. Poor frustrated old sod!
EVELYN. That makes two of you.
CECIL. Evelyn!
EVELYN. You've never thought of anybody but your-

self. You've lived with somebody for fifty years, and not seen that they loved you. You're insensitive and selfish.

CECIL. You don't mean that, Evelyn, do you?

EVELYN. Yes, I do.

CECIL. In that case, it's as well you're not staying.

EVELYN. I daresay.

CECIL. Where are you going?

EVELYN. For a walk along the river.

CECIL. May I come too?

EVELYN. No, no—Cecil. I'd rather be alone.

CECIL. Right. I'll carry on with this. (*She goes, and he resumes his cross-word.* HAWKINS *comes back, black coat or white on again. He resumes work with the tray.*) I hear you're staying, Hawkins.

HAWKINS. Yes, Sir Cecil. If you'll have me.

CECIL. I'll have you, alright. Dammit, I've got nothing else!

HAWKINS. I'm sorry to hear that.

CECIL. Well, that's a change from last night.

HAWKINS. I agree, Sir Cecil. I excuse myself on the grounds that it was a natural reaction. I felt very much unwanted. Then, when I woke up this morning, I thought, "Hawkins, your dreams went out of the window long ago, and they're past fulfilment now. So, why not go along with helping others."

CECIL. Women are a bloody nuisance, that's all I know. Say one thing one minute, and another the next. I don't understand them. All I know is that she got engaged to me last night and came downstairs this morning in reverse gear. How do you explain that?

HAWKINS. I'm in no position to provide an answer, I'm afraid, because, I lack the necessary information about what occurred last night.

CECIL. I lost my head, that's what occurred. I went up to her room and—lost my head.

HAWKINS. Quite understandable, Sir Cecil, in the circumstances.

CECIL. So I've ballsed it up again! The second time in fifty years!! I wish to God I'd never asked her if she wanted a hot-water bottle.

HAWKINS. A hot-water bottle!

CECIL. Yes—when she went up to bed I said, 'If there's not a hot-water bottle in the Blue Room, holler down the stairs.' And, when she did, I took one up.

HAWKINS. But there was one already in the bed.

CECIL. That's not true!!

HAWKINS. Yes, indeed, it is. I placed it there myself, Sir Cecil, after dinner.

CECIL. Good God! But she's not that kind of girl.

HAWKINS. God only made one kind of girl, Sir Cecil.

CECIL. Does it mean she loves me, Hawkins?

HAWKINS. It would seem to point that way, Sir Cecil.

CECIL. Why the devil can't she say so, then?

HAWKINS. A woman moved, as Shakespeare said, is—

CECIL. (*Cutting in.*) Never mind him. Why the devil can't she tell me herself?

HAWKINS. Women have their pride, Sir Cecil.

CECIL. You should know!

HAWKINS. I like to think I have a certain understanding of them, certainly.

CECIL. I wonder—what my chances are now?

HAWKINS. Slim, I'd say, Sir Cecil. (*We hear the front door bell ring.*) That'll be the chauffeur. I'll go and help him load the car, if you'll excuse me.

CECIL. No, no, Hawkins. Hang on till her ladyship comes back from her walk.

HAWKINS. She's not coming back. She wants the car to pick her up at Sutton Place.

CECIL. What! She's gone down there?

HAWKINS. So I understand.

CECIL. To see Jim?

HAWKINS. I believe the object of her visit is to see the Captain, yes.

CECIL. She'll find him in his jodhpurs, Hawkins, wearing spurs and polishing his Range Rover.

HAWKINS. I wouldn't be surprised, Sir Cecil.

CECIL. Cracking whips and blowing hunting horns.

HAWKINS. No doubt, Sir Cecil.

CECIL. And that means I've had it, Hawkins. (*The bell rings again.*) You'd better load the car and send the fellow down to Sutton Place and let him drive her away. (HAWKINS *goes.* SIR CECIL *looks straight ahead in gloom—sees something suddenly. He gets up, takes his glasses, moves towards the river, raises them and looks upstream.* EVELYN *comes out—stands across the stage from* CECIL. CECIL *puts his glasses down, turns round and sees her.*) Ah, your car's here.

EVELYN. Yes I know.

CECIL. I've just been looking at the kingfisher.

EVELYN. I saw it too, I must have frightened it.

CECIL. Well. (*He turns away.*) Give my love to Andover.

EVELYN. Cecil?

CECIL. Yes?

EVELYN. I just caught Jim.

CECIL. Caught him!

EVELYN. He was schooling horses.

CECIL. Oh—it must be one of his good days. (*She laughs. He turns back.*)

EVELYN. You're a wicked old man, Cecil. I've been laughing all along the river. (*She moves towards him.*) May I borrow those?

CECIL. Why?

EVELYN. We might find the kingfisher again. (*She goes—he follows.*)

THE CURTAIN FALLS

Also By
William Douglas Home

THE JOCKEY CLUB STAKES
LLOYD GEORGE KNEW MY FATHER

SAMUELFRENCH.COM

OTHER TITLES AVAILABLE FROM SAMUEL FRENCH

PERFECT WEDDING
Robin Hawdon

Comedy / 2m, 4f / Interior

A man wakes up in the bridal suite on his wedding morning to find an extremely attractive naked girl in bed beside him. In the depths of a stag night hangover, he can't even remember meeting her. Before he can get her out, his bride to be arrives to dress for the wedding. In the ensuing panic, the girl is locked in the bathroom. The best man is persuaded to claim her, but he gets confused and introduces the chamber maid to the bride as his date. The crisis escalates to nuclear levels by the time the mother of the bride and the best man's actual girlfriend arrive. This rare combination of riotous farce and touching love story has provoked waves of laughter across Europe and America.

"Laughs abound."
– *Wisconsin Advocate*

"The full house audience roared with delight."
– *Green Bay Gazette*

SAMUELFRENCH.COM

OTHER TITLES AVAILABLE FROM SAMUEL FRENCH

THREE YEARS FROM "THIRTY"
Mike O'Malley

Comic Drama / 4m, 3f / Unit set
This funny, poignant story of a group of 27-year-olds who have known each other since college sold out during its limited run at New York City's Sanford Meisner Theater. Jessica Titus, a frustrated actress living in Boston, has become distraught over local job opportunities and she is feeling trapped in her long standing relationship with her boyfriend Tom. She suddenly decides to pursue her dreams in New York City. Unbeknownst to her, Tom plans to propose on the evening she has chosen to leave him. The ensuing conflict ripples through their lives and the lives of their roommates and friends, leaving all of them to reconsider their careers, the paths of their souls and the questions, demands and definition of commitment.

SAMUELFRENCH.COM

www.ingramcontent.com/pod-product-compliance
Lightning Source LLC
Chambersburg PA
CBHW070650300426
44111CB00013B/2351